Now *That* Makes Sense!

Relating to People with Wit and Wisdom

To Jim /
Best Wish
From our Comm
Spell Amoitre
To Amoitre

A WISE OWL BOOK

Now
That
Makes
Sense!

Relating to People
with Wit and Wisdom

Compiled by

Mark Ortman

WISE OWL BOOKS
P.O. Box 621
Kirkland, WA 98083
(206) 822-9699

ISBN 0-9634699-9-1

Revised Edition
Second Printing

Cover Design: Gita Endore & Michael Davis

Manufactured in the United States of America

Acknowledgments

I would like to thank the many people involved in making this book possible: to my students who taught me so much about human nature, my brother Paul who introduced me to the world of publishing, Gita Endore for sharing her experience and artistic talents, Linda Ruljancich for reminding me to relax during those hectic moments, Kathleen Kazinsky for the late night reviewing and helping me put my ideas into words, Brian Templeton for his skillful editing and helpful suggestions and of course, all my friends and family for their patience and encouragement.

A special thanks to all the contributors of the quotations in this book, for it is their brilliant insights and observations about life that made this collection possible.

Dedicated to a teacher's teacher,

Al West

Introduction

One evening in 1981, I rummaged across an old book of quotations my brother left behind in storage. I blew off the dust, opened the book, and a few hours later left feeling much wiser and thoroughly entertained.

Now, over ten years later, I often use aphorisims in my work as a teacher, speaker, and business consultant. As Michel de Montaigne once said, "I quote others only to better express myself." I'm always looking for more effective ways to voice my ideas to a wide variety of people, and find those ideas are often better- received when supported by someone else's wit or wisdom. Quotations can spark an awareness of the link between personal experiences and life's larger patterns. This helps support and reinforce my message in an effort to be clear and persuasive.

The quotations in this book focus on ideas about human relations. It seems much of our lives are spent communicating with others, with far too little knowledge of effective approaches. Many of life's greatest challenges involve our relationships and dealings with people. My intent here is to provide an entertaining and informative communication resource.

I have indexed this collection three ways for your

convenience: First, subjects are listed alphabetically for quick reference. Then, a cross-reference of subjects listed under one of five headings: About People, Difficulties with People, Changing People's Minds, Ways of Expressing Ourselves and Showing Gratitude. Finally, a complete authors' index at the back of the book.

The contents in this book have been drawn from a variety of sources and personal experiences throughout the years. Every attempt has been made to give credit to the originators of the quotations. Where I failed to give proper credit, future printings will include changes that are brought to my attention.

Use this book to entertain, educate, persuade, be a resource for your newsletter, training program, writings, or presentations. As my friend and mentor has said, "Take the best and leave the rest." I hope you enjoy this collection and find it to be as useful as I have.

Your comments or additional quotations relating to people are welcomed and with your permission they may be used in future publications.

Mark Ortman
Seattle, 1992

Alphabetical Listing of Subjects

Advice   14

Appreciation   19

Arguments   22

Asking Questions   29

Being Honest   35

Character   38

Complainers   41

Compliments   44

Compromising   47

Conversation   49

Criticism   54

Difficult People   58

Diplomacy   68

Ego/Egotist   70

Encouragement   73

Fault-Finding   77

Flattery   81

Getting Angry   83

Golden Rule   90

Gossip   92

Human Nature   95

Influencing Others   103

Insults   109

Kindness   111

Listening   116

Negotiation   125

Non-Verbal Communication   132

Opinions   135

People/Personality   141

Persuasiveness   148

Placing Blame   156

Praise   158

Public Speaking   162

Resolving Conflict   167

Self-Interest   175

Silence   180

Smiling   185

Tact   187

Talking   191

Truthfulness   199

Trust   205

Wit   207

Words   210

Cross-Reference of Subjects

About People...

Character	38
Ego/Egotist	70
Human Nature	95
People/Personality	141
Self-Interest	175
Trust	205

Difficulties With People...

Arguments	22
Complainers	41
Criticism	54
Difficult People	58
Fault-Finding	77
Getting Angry	83
Gossip	92

Insults 109

Placing Blame 156

Resolving Conflict 167

Changing People's Minds...

Advice 14

Compromising 47

Diplomacy 68

Influencing Others 103

Negotiation 125

Persuasiveness 148

Tact 187

Ways of Expressing Ourselves...

Asking Questions 29

Conversation 49

Being Honest 35

Listening 116

Non-Verbal Communication   132

Opinions   135

Public Speaking   162

Silence   180

Smiling   185

Talking   191

Truthfulness   199

Wit   207

Words   210

Showing Gratitude...

Appreciation   19

Compliments   47

Encouragement   73

Flattery   81

Golden Rule   90

Kindness   111

Praise   158

Don't think people judge your generosity by the amount of advice you give away.

Anonymous

We advise others in areas we have difficulty advising ourselves.

Anonymous

I give good advice with the same enthusiasm and sincerity in which I give bad advice.

Unknown

Do not offer advice which has not been seasoned by your own performance.

Henry S. Haskins

Never trust the advice of a man in difficulties.

Aesop

Some people know a lot more than they're willing to tell. Unfortunately, the reverse is true.

Anonymous

When I transfer my knowledge, I teach. When I transfer my beliefs, I indoctrinate.

Arthur Danto

Advice is like snow; the softer it falls, the deeper it sinks into the mind.

Samuel Taylor Coleridge

An idea isn't responsible for the people who believe it.

Don Marquis

Advice is like kissing; it costs nothing and is a pleasant thing to do.
Josh Billings

Distrust interested advice.

> Aesop

As for me, all I know is nothing.

> Socrates

Everyone tells you to have a nice day but nobody
tells you how.

> Anonymous

Don't accept that others know you better than
yourself.

> Sonya Friedman

"Be yourself" is often the worse advice you can
give people.

> Tom Masson

I have found the best way to give advice to people is to find out what they want and then advise them to do it.

Harry Truman

No one wants advice, only corroboration.

John Steinbeck

A good scare is worth more to a man than good advice.

E. W. Howe

Old men are fond of giving advice to console themselves for being no longer in a position to give bad examples.

La Rochefoucauld

One can give advice comfortably from a safe port.

Friedrich von Schiller

No man is wise enough to be another's master.

Edward Abby

It is always a silly thing to give advice, but to give bad advice is fatal.

Oscar Wilde

Good rarely came from good advice.

Lord Byron

Nobody really knows nothing.

Mark Ortman

I expect that all of us get pretty much what we deserve of appreciation.

A. C. Benson

No person was ever honored for what he received; honor has been the reward for what he has given.

Calvin Coolidge

Who does not thank for little will not thank for much.

Estonian Proverb

There is one word which may serve as a rule of practice for all one's life - reciprocity.

Confucius

Happiness is a by-product of an effort to make someone else happy.

Gretta Palmer

Blessed is he who expects no gratitude, for he shall not be disappointed.

W. C. Bennett

Do not save your loving speeches for your friends till they are dead.

Anna Cummins

Gratitude takes three forms: a feeling in the heart, an expression in words, and a giving in return.

Anonymous

The greatest humiliation in life is to work hard on something from which you expect great appreciation, and then fail to get it.

E. W. Howe

I now perceive one immense omission in my psychology - the deepest principle of human nature is the craving to be appreciated.

> William James

Man lives more by affirmation than by bread.

> Victor Hugo

Three-fourths of the people you will ever meet are hungering and thirsting for appreciation. Give it to them and they will love you.

> Dale Carnegie

One of the deepest secrets of life is that all that is really worth doing is what we do for others.

> Lewis Carroll

Strife is better than loneliness.

Irish Proverb

One of the hardest things in this world to do is to admit you are wrong. And nothing is more helpful in resolving an argument than its frank admission.

Benjamin Disraeli

Arguing is a game two can play at. But it is a strange game in that neither opponent ever wins.

Benjamin Franklin

A chip on the shoulder is a sure indication that there is more wood higher up.

Aldous Huxley

The best way to answer a bad argument is to let it go on.

Sydney Smith

Silence is one of the hardest kind of arguments to refute.

Josh Billings

There is one thing to be said for ignorance - it sure causes a lot of interesting arguments.

Anonymous

Never argue with a fool; people might not know the difference.

Anonymous

He who establishes his argument by noise and command shows that his reason is weak.

Michel de Montaigne

Arguments

I never saw an instance of one of two disputants convincing the other by argument.

Thomas Jefferson

My idea of an agreeable person is a person who agrees with me.

Benjamin Disraeli

Whenever two people argue over principles, they are both right.

Marie Von Eschenbach

The best argument is that which seems merely like an explanation.

Dale Carnegie

Argument is a great substitute for thinking.

Mark Ortman

Temper is what gets most of us in an argument. Pride is what keeps us there.

Anonymous

Arguments thrive on opposition and die without it.

Anonymous

People who fight with fire usually end up in ashes.

Abigail Van Buren

When in an argument, try asking questions instead of making statements.

Unknown

When one will not, two can not quarrel.

Proverb

Arguments

Any fact is better established by two or three good testimonies than by a thousand arguments.

Nathanial Emmons

A long dispute means both parties are wrong.

Voltaire

Behind every argument is someone's ignorance.

Louis D. Brandeis

If you are ignorant, you certainly can get into some pretty interesting arguments.

Herbert Prochow

Prejudice not founded on reason cannot be removed by argument.

Samuel Johnson

You can easily play a joke on a man who likes to argue; agree with him.

> E. W. Howe

The best way I know to win an argument is to start out by being right.

> Lord Hailsham

How many a dispute could have been deflated if the disputants had dared to define their terms.

> Aristotle

Rediscover the foundation of truth and the purpose and cause of dispute immediately disappear.

> Louis D. Brandeis

The quickest way to kindle a fire is to rub two opposing opinions together.

> Anonymous

He who strikes the first blow admits he's lost the argument.

Chinese Proverb

The aim of an argument or discussion should not be victory, but progress.

Joseph Joubert

Soft words make hard arguments.

Thomas Fuller

There is no sense in having an argument with a man so stupid he doesn't know you have the better of him.

Samuel Johnson

I always get the better when I argue alone.

Oliver Goldsmith

To be able to ask a question clearly is two-thirds of the way to getting the answer.

John Ruskin

We should not only use the brain we have, but all that we can borrow.

Woodrow Wilson

There are two sides to every question, one which we're not especially interested in.

Anonymous

You never have to know all the answers because you won't be asked all the questions.

Herbert Prochnow

Many things are lost for want of not asking.

English Proverb

Better to ask twice than to lose your way once.

Danish Proverb

It is less embarrassing to ask a silly question than to explain later why you didn't.

Anonymous

The true mark of a well-educated man is that he never tries to answer a question before being asked to do so.

Anonymous

Know how to ask. There is nothing more difficult for some people, nor for others, easier.

Baltasar Gracian

Why must the phrase "it is none of my business" always be followed by the word "but"?

Milwaukee Journal

He who has all the answers hasn't heard all the questions.

Anonymous

Don't ask questions if you don't want to hear the answers.

Anonymous

More gold has been mined from the minds of men than has ever been taken from the earth.

Unknown

There aren't any embarrassing questions, only embarrassing answers.

Carl Rowan

To question a wise man is the beginning of wisdom.

German Proverb

Judge a man by his questions, not his answers.

Voltaire

When you hear a half-truth, find the other half.

Anonymous

I keep six honest serving men... they taught me everything I know; their names are: what and why and when and how and who and where.

Rudyard Kipling

There are three sides to every question: your side, his side, and to hell with it.

Anonymous

Don't ask questions of fairy tales.

Jewish Proverb

Not every question deserves an answer.

Publilius Syrus

Before one replies, one must be present.

African Proverb

Getting information from him was like squeezing a third cup from a tea bag.

Christopher Buckley

One by one, neatly, like index cards out of a machine, the little questions dropped.

Ronald Dahl

Why is it that when people say "that's a good question" they never have a good answer?

Walter J. Kennevan

No question is so difficult to answer as one in which the answer is obvious.

George Bernard Shaw

He must be very ignorant, for he answers every question he is asked.
Voltaire

A prudent question is one half of wisdom.

Francis Bacon

It is easier to judge a person's mental capacity by his questions than by his answers.

Le Duc de Levis

The first key to wisdom is constant and frequent questioning... for by doubting we are led to questioning and by questioning we arrive at the truth.
Peter Aberlard

The genius of communication is the ability to be honest and kind at the same time.

John Powell

People who are brutally honest get more satisfaction out of the brutality than out of the honesty.

Richard J. Needham

To be honest, one must be inconsistent.

H.G. Wells

He is such an honest man, you could shoot craps with him over the phone.

Earl Wilson

Absolute honesty is as absurd an abstraction as an absolute temperature or an absolute value.

George Bernard Shaw

It is useless to try to hold some people to anything they say while they're madly in love,
drunk, or running for office.

Anonymous

A good portion of speaking will consist in knowing how to lie.

Desiderius Erasmus

Exaggeration is a branch of lying.

Baltasar Gracian

A little inaccuracy saves a world of explanation.

C. E. Ayres

Honesty pays, but it doesn't seem to pay enough
to suit some people.
Kin Hubbard

You don't tell deliberate lies, but sometimes you have to be evasive.

Margaret Thatcher

A lie with a purpose is one of the worst kind, and the most profitable.

Josh Billings

There are times when lying is the most sacred of duties.

Eugene Marian Labiche

Ask me no questions and I'll tell you no fibs.

Oliver Goldsmith

Men are always sincere. They change sinceri-ties, that's all.

Tristan Bernard

One of the best ways to measure people is to watch the way they behave when something is free.

Ann Landers

The measure of a man's character is what he would do if he knew he would never be found out.

Thomas B. Macaulay

The final test of a gentleman is his respect for those who can be of no possible service to him.

William Lyon Phelps

Every man has three characters: that which he exhibits, that which he has, and that which he thinks he has.

Alphonse Karr

People are like stained glass windows. They sparkle and shine when the sun is out, but when darkness sets in, their true beauty is revealed only if there is light from within.

Elizabeth Kubler-Ross

Character does not change. Opinions alter, but character is only developed.

Benjamin Disraeli

I begin to find that too good a character is inconvenient.

Sir Walter Scott

When a man thinks he is reading the character of another, he is often unconsciously betraying his own.

Joseph Farrell

By nothing do men show their character more than by the things they laugh at.

Goethe

We must have a weak spot or two in our character before we can love others much.

Oliver Wendell Holmes

A character is like an acrostic... read it forward, backward, or across, it spells the same thing.

Ralph Waldo Emerson

Personality has the power to open many doors, but it's character that keeps them open.

Anonymous

Character is what you have left when you've lost everything you can lose.

Evan Esar

The next time you feel like complaining, remember your garbage disposal probably eats better than 30% of the people in the world.

Robert Orben

He that always complains is never pitied.

Anonymous

I complained because I had no shoes until I met a man with no feet.
Arabic Proverb

Make it a habit to economize on the time spent complaining.
Anonymous

Don't tell other people your troubles. Half of them aren't interested and the other half are glad you got what you had coming to you.

Anonymous

Complainers

There is something wrong with a man, as a
motor, when he knocks continually.

Anonymous

The wheel that squeaks the loudest is the one
that gets all the grease.

Josh Billings

It is a popular error to suppose that the loudest
complainers about the public are the most anxious for its welfare.

Edmund Burke

The trouble with this country is that there are
too many people going about saying "the trouble
with this country is..."

Sinclair Lewis

Before the squeaky wheel gets the grease, check first to see if it isn't just spinning.

Chuck Werk

Everyone complains of his memory, but no one complains of his judgement.

La Rochefoucauld

Can anybody remember when times were not hard, and money not scarce?

Ralph Waldo Emerson

The wheel that squeaks the loudest is the first to be replaced.
Anonymous

Constant complaint is the poorest sort of pay for all the comforts we enjoy.

Benjamin Franklin

Compliments

Some folks pay a compliment like they went down in their pocket for it.

          Kin Hubbard

A compliment is a little touch of love surrounded by a great imagination.

          Emile Taquet

Look for strength in people, not weakness; good, not evil. Most of us find what we search for.

          Anonymous

You do have the right to be generous. If he has the spirit of true generosity, a pauper can give like a prince.

          Corrine V. Wells

There is nothing you can say in answer to a compliment. I have been complimented myself a great many times, and they always embarrass me. I always feel they have not said enough.

Mark Twain

I can live for two months on a good compliment.

Mark Twain

Some fellows pay a compliment like they expected a receipt.
Kin Hubbard

We praise or blame according to whether the one or the other offers a greater opportunity for our power of judgment to shine out.

Friedrich Nietzsche

Compliments

A liar is not hard to believe when he says nice
things about you.

Anonymous

Most of us can run pretty well all day on one
good compliment.

Anonymous

One kind word can warm three winter nights.

Japanese Proverb

If you can't get a compliment any other way, pay
yourself one.

Mark Twain

Do not be too hasty in accusing or approving
anyone.

Publilius Syrus

The world may be divided into those who take it or leave it and those who split the difference.

Ronald Knox

Compromise without resentment is the key to living together.

Henry Rabin

Sometimes the best gain is to lose.

Proverb

A compromise is the art of dividing a cake in such a way everyone believes that he has the biggest piece.

Ludwig Erhard

Better bend than break.

Scottish Proverb

Compromising

Compromise is but the sacrifice of one right or good in the hope of retaining another; too often ending in the loss of both.

Tyrone Edwards

It is not who is right, but what is right.

Anonymous

Every human benefit and enjoyment, every virtue, and every prudent act, is founded on compromise and barter.
Edmund Burke

Life cannot subsist in society but by reciprocal concessions.
Samuel Johnson

It is futile to linger endlessly over differences; the fruitful research is to look for points of contact.

A. G. Sertillanges

Conversation is something that starts the moment after you put your foot through the television tube.

> Anonymous

One evening's conversation with a superior man is better than ten years of study.

> Chinese Proverb

The real art of conversation is not only to say the right thing in the right place, but to leave unsaid the wrong thing in a tempting moment.

> Dorothy Nevill

The American's conversation is much like courtship... he gives an inkling and watches for a reaction. If the weather looks fair, he inkles a little more.

> Donald Lloyd

Conversation

We always deeply resent the person at a party who, while he speaks with us, keeps his eyes roving around the room as if in search of someone bigger and better to talk to.

Dorothy Walworth

Storytelling reveals meaning without committing the error of defining it.

Hannah Arendt

If you tell a good story, its narration will remind hearers of a bad one.

E. W. Howe

One of the best rules in conversation is never to say a thing which any of the company can reasonably wish had been left unsaid.

Jonathan Swift

Conversation is a verbal exchange of 90% talking and 10% listening.

Evan Esar

If wiseman's way you wisely seek, five things observe with care: of whom you speak, to whom you speak, and how, and when, and where.

Anonymous

If every man were straightforward in his opinions, there would be no conversation.

Benjamin Disraeli

Conversation would be vastly improved by the constant use of four simple words; " I do not know."

Andre Maurois

Conversation

Silence is the great art of conversation.

William Hazlitt

Conversation is when three people are talking; gossip is when one of them leaves.

Anonymous

A gossip is one who talks about others; a bore is one who talks about himself; and a brilliant conversationalist is one who talks to you about yourself.

Lisa Kirk

That is the happiest conversation where there is no competition, no vanity, but calm, quiet interchange of sentiments.

Samuel Johnson

Debate is the death of conversation.

Emil Ludwig

Never speak of yourself to others; make them talk about themselves instead. Therein lies the whole art of conversation.

Jules de Goncourt

The reason why so few people are agreeable in conversation is that each is thinking more about what he intends to say than about what the other is saying.

La Rochefoucauld

Good nature is more agreeable in conversation than wit, and gives a certain expression to the face which is more amiable than beauty.

George Ade

He has the right to criticize who has the heart to help.

Abraham Lincoln

Pay no attention to what a critic says. No statue was ever put up for a critic.

Jean Sibelius

The person who says it cannot be done should not interrupt the person doing it.

Chinese Proverb

A critic is a man who knows the way, but can't drive the car.

Kenneth Tynan

It is much easier to be critical than correct.

Benjamin Disraeli

A never-failing way to get rid of a fellow is to tell him something for his own good.

Kin Hubbard

Criticism is most effective when it sounds like praise.

Anonymous

He who listens to what people say of him shall never have peace.

Proverb

Don't mind criticism. If it is untrue, disregard it. If it is unfair, keep from irritation. If it is ignorant, smile. If it is justified, learn from it.

Unknown

A good cure for a critical spirit is an honest look at ourselves, not at others.

Anonymous

Criticism

We must not allow other people's limited percep-
tions to define us.

Virginia Satir

If you stop every time a dog barks, your road will
never end.

Arabian Proverb

Do not remove a fly from your friend's forehead
with a hatchet.

Chinese Proverb

Do not fear when your enemies criticize you.
Beware when they applaud.

Vo Dong Giang

When you hear A criticize B, you learn more
about A.

Paul Dickson

Mud thrown is lost ground.

Proverb

Never look down on people unless you are helping them up.
Jesse Jackson

The strength of criticism lies in the weakness of the thing being criticized.

Henry W. Longfellow

The tongue is the deadliest of all blunt instruments.
Anonymous

Remember that nobody will ever get ahead of you as long as he is kicking you in the seat of the pants.

Walter Winchell

Difficult People

Doesn't it seem some days as though other people were put in the world for no other reason than to aggravate you?

E. W. Howe

I don't have any trouble regulating my own conduct, but keeping other folks straight is what bothers me.

Josh Billings

I have learned silence from the talkative, toleration from the intolerant, and kindness from the unkind; yet strange, I am ungrateful to these teachers.

Kahlil Gibran

If you have been put in your place long enough, you begin to act like the place.

Randall Jarrell

Nothing is so hard to do so gracefully as getting off your high horse.

> Franklin P. Jones

What is slander? A verdict of "guilty" pronounced in the absence of the accused, behind closed doors, without defense or appeal, by a prejudiced judge.

> Joseph Roux

Keep the other person's well-being in mind when you feel an attack of soul-purging truth coming on.

> Betty White

Nobody has a right to put another under such difficulty that he must either hurt the person by telling the truth, or hurt himself by telling what is not true.

> Samuel Johnson

It is better to cause happiness where you go
than to cause happiness when you go.

Anonymous

People who think they know it all annoy those of
us who already do.

Anonymous

As long as people will accept crap, it will be
profitable to dispense it.

Dick Cavett

Misery no longer loves company; nowadays it
insists on it.

Russell Baker

Firmness is that admirable quality in ourselves
that is merely stubborness in others.

Anonymous

It is always easier to hate something than to understand it.

Anonymous

If you act like an ass, don't get insulted if people ride you.

Yiddish Proverb

There are none so empty as those who are so full of themselves.

Benjamin Whichcote

A man never tells you anything until you contradict him.

George Bernard Shaw

We never forgive those who make us blush.

Jean de La Harpe

Those who hate you don't win unless you hate them back; then you destroy yourself.

Richard Nixon

The trouble with being pleasant is people think you're a hypocrite.

Franklin P. Jones

Hate is like acid. It can not only destroy the vessel in which it is stored, but also destroy the object on which it is poured.

Ann Landers

Age has nothing to do with learning a new way to be stupid.

J. C. Salak

Never underestimate the power of human stupidity.

Robert Heinlein

When somebody does something for your own good, you can bet you're not going to enjoy it.

Doug Larson

Most of the trouble in the world is caused by people wanting to be important.

T. S. Eliot

Most people would sooner die than think, and often do.

Bertrand Russell

The difference between a conviction and a prejudice is that you can explain a conviction without getting angry.

Anonymous

People with the narrowest minds always seem to have the widest mouths.

Anonymous

Be aware that a halo has to fall only a few inches to be a noose.

Dan McKinnon

If you argue and rankle and contradict, you may achieve a victory sometimes; but it will be an empty victory because you will never get your opponent's good will.

Benjamin Franklin

Most of us like people who come right out and say what they think, unless they disagree with us.

Anonymous

Half our mistakes in life arise from feeling when we ought to be thinking, and thinking when we ought to be feeling.

John Churton Collins

Too often, the person who takes his time, takes yours too.

Anonymous

If you say what you think, don't expect to hear what you like.

Malcolm Forbes

A dog has a lot of friends and fun, maybe because he wags his tail and not his tongue.

Anonymous

Our strength as humans is that we can laugh at ourselves for being ridiculous. Our weakness is that we have to do it so often.

Unknown

It often happens that a man is more humanely related to a cat or dog than to any human being.

Henry David Thoreau

Difficult People

The human race has been able to improve everything but people.

> Anonymous

A closed mouth gathers no feet.

> Proverb

If they don't throw it, you can't hit it.

> Lefty Gomez

Better slip with foot than with tongue.

> Proverb

Let not your tongue say what your head may pay for.

> Italian Proverb

Man is the only animal that can remain on friendly terms with the victim he intends to eat.

Samuel Butler

Man is always as wicked as his needs require.

Giacomo Leopardi

I know that there are people in this world who do not love their fellow human beings, and I hate people like that.

Tom Lehrer

Even a lion has to defend himself against flies.

German Proverb

I have more trouble with D.L. Moody than any other man I know.

D. L. Moody

Diplomacy is the art of saying things in such a way that those to whom we speak may listen to them with pleasure.

Blaise Pascal

The difference between being diplomatic and undiplomatic is the difference between saying "when I look at you, time stands still", and saying "your face would stop a clock".

Unknown

A diplomat is anyone who thinks twice before saying nothing.

Anonymous

A diplomat is a person who can tell you to go to hell in such a way that you actually look forward to the trip.

Caskie Stinnett

Diplomacy is the art of letting someone else have your way.

Anonymous

If tact doesn't work, try diplomacy.

Anonymous

To say nothing, especially when speaking, is half the art of diplomacy.

Will Durant

Diplomacy is to do and say the nastiest things in the nicest way.

Isaac Goldberg

Subtlety is the art of saying what you think and getting out of range before it is understood.

Anonymous

Ego/Egotist

An egotist is a person of low taste, more
interested in himself than me.

Ambrose Bierce

When a man is wrapped up in himself, he makes
a pretty small package.

John Ruskin

Every man is of importance to himself.

Samuel Johnson

Never to talk about oneself is a very refined form
of hypocrisy.

Friedrich Nietzsche

He that falls in love with himself will have no
rivals.

Benjamin Franklin

The great act of faith is when a man decides he
is not God.

> Oliver Wendell Holmes

A strong ego is nature's way of compensating for
mediocrity.

> L. A. Safian

An egotist is a person who thinks that if he
hadn't been born, people would have wondered
why.

> Dan Post

One nice thing about egotists: they don't talk
about other people.

> Lucille S. Harper

A vain man can never be utterly ruthless. He
wants to win applause, and therefore he accom-
modates himself to others.

> Goethe

An egotist is someone me deep in conversation.

Anonymous

It is real hard to think of yourself as the center of the universe with a finger up your nose.

C. W. Metcalf

An egotist is one who suffers from "I" strain.

Anonymous

Conceit is God's gift to little men.

Bruce Barton

Ego: the only thing that keeps growing without nourishment.

Evan Esar

All we can ever do in the way of good to people is to encourage them to do good for themselves.

Randolph Bourne

To teach a man how he may learn to grow independently, and for himself, is perhaps the greatest service that one man can do for another.

Benjamin Jowett

If you call a thing bad you do little; if you call a thing good you do much.

Goethe

The best way to help people to overcome their weak points is to do what you can to encourage and develop their strong points.

Unknown

Encouragement

We have enough people who tell it like it is - now
we could use a few who tell it like it can be.

Robert Orben

He that does good to another does good also to
himself.

Seneca

If you treat an individual as if he were what he
ought to be and could be, he will become what
he ought to be and could be.

Goethe

The best way to cheer yourself up is to try to
cheer someone else up.

Mark Twain

When someone does something good, applaud!
That will make two people happy.

Samuel Goldwyn

Never discourage anyone who continually makes progress, no matter how slow.

Plato

Tell a man he is brave, and you help him become so.

Thomas Carlyle

The best way to knock a chip off your neighbor's shoulder is to pat him on the back.

Anonymous

Good words cost nothing, but are worth much.

Anonymous

If someone were to pay you ten cents for every kind word you ever spoke and collect five cents for every unkind word, would you be rich or poor?

Unknown

Encouragement

A bit of fragrance always clings to the hand that gives you roses.

Chinese Proverb

A word of encouragement during failure is worth more than a dictionary of praise after success.

Anonymous

You can't help a man uphill without getting closer to the top yourself.

Proverb

Encourage all sincere attempts at achievement, no matter how modest; for sometimes great achievements start from modest beginnings.

Unknown

People with no faults are terrible; there is no way of taking advantage of them.

Anatole France

Many people believe that admitting a fault means they no longer have to correct it.

Marie Von Eschenbach

Criticism is the disapproval of people not for having faults, but for having faults different from our own.

Anonymous

If you hear that someone is speaking ill of you, instead of trying to defend yourself, say: "Obviously he does not know me very well since there are so many other faults he could have mentioned".

Epictetus

Fault-Finding

Better a diamond with flaws than a pebble
without.
> Confucius

Our faults irritate us most when we see them in
others.

> Anonymous

Wouldn't it be nice if we could find other things
as easily as we find fault.

> Anonymous

If we had no faults, we would not take so much
pleasure in noting those of others.

> La Rochefoucauld

Gladly we desire to make other men perfect, but
we will not amend our own fault.

> Thomas a' Kempis

Most of us can live peacefully with our own faults, but the faults of others get on our nerves.

Anonymous

Be patient with the faults of others; they have to be patient with yours.

Anonymous

Clean your fingers before you point at my spots.

Benjamin Franklin

There is nothing that will kill a man so soon as having nobody to find fault with but himself.

George Eliot

If you are pleased with finding faults, you are displeased at finding perfections.

Johann Kaspar Lavater

Fault-Finding

Faults tend to be thick where love is thin.

Anonymous

There are spots even on the sun.

Proverb

Love your enemies, for they tell you your faults.

Benjamin Franklin

Deal with the faults of others as gently as your own.

Chinese Proverb

The greatest of faults, I should say, is to be conscious of none.

Thomas Carlyle

Flattery rarely hurts a man unless he inhales.

Anonymous

What really flatters a man is that you think him worth flattering.

George Bernard Shaw

Flattery is like chewing gum... enjoy it briefly, but don't swallow it.

Anonymous

Be advised that all flatterers live at the expense of those who listen to them.

Jean de La Fontaine

Many men know how to flatter, few men know how to praise.

Greek Proverb

Flattery

Flattery is like counterfeit money which, but for vanity, would have no circulation.

La Rochefoucauld

The best way to flatter a man is to tell him he's the kind of person who can't be flattered.

Anonymous

A flatterer is one who says things to your face that he wouldn't say behind your back.

Anonymous

Flattery is a form of soft soap, and soft soap is mostly made of lye.
Evan Esar

He that flatters you more than you desire either has deceived you or wishes to deceive you.

Italian Proverb

If you want to hear the whole truth about yourself, anger your neighbor.

Anonymous

It is my rule never to lose my temper till it would be detrimental to keep it.

Sean O'Casey

You don't get rid of your temper when you lose it.
Proverb

Never forget what a man says to you while he is angry.
Thomas Fuller

Many a man's profanity has saved him from a nervous breakdown.
Henry S. Haskins

Getting Angry

A life based on reason will always require to be balanced by an occasional bout of violent and irrational emotion, for the instinctual drives must be satisfied.

Cyril Connolly

Too many people work up a head of steam before they find out what's cooking.

Anonymous

If you are patient in one moment of anger, you will escape a hundred days of sorrow.

Chinese Proverb

Anyone who angers you, conquers you.

Sister Kenny's Mother

If you are angry, people will focus on your anger instead of your problem.

Stephen Pollan

Swallowing angry words is much easier than having to eat them.

Grit

The greatest cure for anger is delay.

Seneca

When a person goes on a diet the first thing he loses is his temper.

Anonymous

Keep your temper! No one else wants it.

Anonymous

Anger is the wind that blows out the light of reason.

Robert Ingersoll

Getting Angry

Inquire not what boils in another's pot.

Thomas Fuller

To obtain a man's opinion of you, make him angry.

Oliver Wendell Holmes

Kindle not a fire you cannot extinquish.

Proverb

Anger always thinks it has power beyond its power.

Publilius Syrus

The peculiarity of ill temper is that it is the vice of the virtuous.

Anonymous

Temper is a funny thing; it spoils children, ruins men, and strengthens steel.

Anonymous

Handle your anger by preventing its build-up.

Dale Galloway

When angry, count four; when very angry, swear.

Mark Twain

We boil at different degrees.

Ralph Waldo Emerson

Anger is one letter short of danger.

Anonymous

Anger... the feeling that makes your mouth work faster than your mind.

> Evan Esar

Anger is never without an argument, but seldom with a good one.

> Lord Halifax

Anger and intolerance are the twin enemies of correct understanding.

> Mahatma Gandhi

An angry man is again angry with himself when he returns to reason.

> Publilius Syrus

What begins in anger ends in shame.

> Benjamin Franklin

Never kick a fresh turd on a hot day.

Harry S. Truman

Anger is a momentary madness, so control your passion or it will control you.

Horace

When a man is wrong and won't admit it, he always gets angry.

Thomas Haliburton

As fire is kindled by bellows, so is anger by words.

English Proverb

Anybody can become angry; that is easy. But to be angry with the right person, and to the right degree, and at the right time, and for the right purpose, and in the right way... this is not within everybody's power and is not easy.

Aristotle

89

All things whatsoever ye would that men should do to you, do ye even so to them: for this is the law of the prophets.

Bible (Christianity)

What is hateful to you, do not to your fellow man. That is the entire law; all the rest is commentary.

Talmud (Judaism)

This is the sum of duty: do naught unto others which would cause you pain if done to you.

Mahabbarata
(Hinduism)

Hurt not others in ways that you yourself would find hurtful.

Udana-Varga
(Buddhism)

Regard your neighbor's gain as your own gain, and your neighbor's loss as your own loss.

T'ai Shang Ying P'ien
(Taoism)

That nature alone is good which refrains from doing unto another whatsoever is not good for itself.

Dadistan-I-Dinik
(Zoroastrianism)

No one of you is a believer until he desires for his brother that which he desires for himself.

Sunnah (Islam)

Surely it is the maxim of loving kindness: do not unto others what you would not have them do unto you.

Analects (Confucianism)

Gossip

Whoever gossips to you will gossip of you.

> Latin Proverb

Conversation is when three people are talking; gossip is when one of them leaves.

> Anonymous

Of what does not concern you, say nothing good or bad.

> Italian Proverb

Gossip is when you hear something you like about someone you don't.

> Earl Wilson

I listened as she poured a little social sewage into his ears.

> George Meredith

There is only one thing in the world worse than being talked about, and that is not being talked about.

Oscar Wilde

There are two kinds of people who blow through life like a breeze: one kind is gossipers, and the other is gossipees.

Ogden Nash

Gossiper... one who gets the best news from somebody who promised to keep it a secret.

Evan Esar

Gossip is the art of saying nothing in a way that leaves practically nothing unsaid.

Walter Winchell

At every word a reputation dies.

Alexander Pope

Gossip

Show me someone who never gossips, and I'll show you someone who isn't interested in people.

Barbara Walters

If all men knew what others say of them, there would not be four friends in the world.

Blaise Pascal

How awful to reflect that what other people say of us is true.

Logan Pearsall Smith

None are so fond of secrets as those who do not intend to keep them.

C. C. Colton

The only fair way to talk about people is to imagine that they are listening to every word you say.

Unknown

I believe in the theory that the strongest motive, whether we are conscious of it or not, rules our conduct.

Ellen Glasgow

Prejudices subsist in people's minds long after they have been destroyed by their experience.

Ernest Dimnet

A satisfied need is no longer a motivator.

Anonymous

Pride and fear kill communication.

Anonymous

Human beings are perhaps never more frightening than when they are convinced beyond a doubt that they are right.

Laurens Van Der Post

Gain does not give as much pleasure as loss gives grief.

>   Greek Proverb

Our necessities are few but our wants are endless.

>   H. W. Shaw

Human nature is something that makes you swear at a pedestrian when you are driving and at a driver when you are pedestrian.

>   Anonymous

Principles have no real force except when one is well fed.

>   Mark Twain

When the stomach is full, it is easy to talk of fasting.

>   St. Jerome

No man does anything from a single motive.

Samuel Taylor Coleridge

A man can only understand what is akin to something already existing in himself.

Henry F. Amiel

The best way to study human nature is when nobody else is present.

Thomas L. Masson

There is no way to take the danger out of human relationships.

Barbara G. Harrison

We are slaves to whatever we don't understand.

Vernon Howard

There is neither good or bad, but thinking
makes it so.

William Shakespeare

Our senses are the camera lens through which
we view the world. Our point of view is limited to
what our perspective sees.

Unknown

Nobody realizes that some people expend
tremendous energy merely to be normal.

Albert Camus

The deepest urge in human nature is the desire
to be important.

John Dewey

Three human faults or deficiencies: laziness,
selfishness and thoughtlessness.

Unknown

The three main human drives are for identity, stimulation and security... in that order.

Robert Ardrey

The average person has five senses: touch, taste, smell, sight and hearing. The genius has two more... horse and common.

Anonymous

One is vain by nature... modest by necessity.

Pierre Reverdy

Man is made by his beliefs. As he believes, so he is.

Bhagavad Gita

Human nature tends to identify with the role of those it sympathizes with or fears.

Anonymous

Human nature has only two primal passions: to get and to beget.

Sir William Olser

How many natures lie in human nature?

Blaise Pascal

Work keeps us from three great evils: boredom, vice and need.

Voltaire

Human being... an embodied paradox, a bundle of contradictions.

C. C. Colton

People can be divided into two classes: those who go ahead and do something and those who sit still and inquire, "Why wasn't it done the other way?"

Oliver Wendell Holmes

He who makes great demands on himself is naturally inclined to make great demands on others.

Andre Gide

Those who love to be feared, fear to be loved. Some fear them, but they fear everyone.

Jean Pierre Camus

No man is a hypocrite in his pleasure.

Samuel Johnson

Everybody is ignorant, only on different subjects.

Will Rogers

All human actions have one or more of these seven causes: chance, nature, compulsion, habit, reason, passion or desire.

Aristotle

We hate what we fear, and so where hate is, fear is lurking.

Cyril Connolly

We do not walk on our legs, but on our will.

Sufi Proverb

Men's natures are alike; it is their habits that carry them apart.

Confucius

Habit is stronger than reason.

George Santayana

Every heart has its own ache.

Proverb

You can exert no influence if you are not
susceptible to influence.
Carl G. Jung

One of the things a man has to fight most
bitterly is the influence of those who love him.

Sherwood Anderson

Influence is something you have until you try to
use it.
Anonymous

Be it true or false, what is said about people
often has as much influence upon their lives, and
especially upon their destinies, as what they do.

Victor Hugo

Human beings are not influenced by anything to
which they are not naturally disposed.

Hesketh Pearson

There is a road from the eye to the heart that does not go through the intellect.

G. K. Chesterton

The master said: "Without knowing the force of words, it is impossible to know men."

Confucius

Too much politeness conceals deceit.

Chinese Proverb

We cannot overhaul the mind of the listener, but we can waltz with his feelings and emotions.

Anonymous

A leader is a man who has the ability to get other people to do what they don't want to do and like it.

Harry S. Truman

Tell me and I'll forget; show me and I may remember; involve me and I'll understand.

Chinese Proverb

Once you get people laughing, they're listening, and you can tell them almost anything.

Herb Gardner

It is not enough to conquer; one must know how to seduce.

Voltaire

You have not converted a man because you have silenced him.

John Morley

When you speak to other people for their own good, it is influence; and when other people speak to you for your own good, it is interference.

Anonymous

To know how to suggest is the great art of teaching.

Ralph Waldo Emerson

Conduct is more convincing than language.

John Woolman

What is necessary to change a person is to change his awareness of himself.

Abraham H. Maslow

You cannot lead anyone further than you have gone.

Proverb

Consider how hard it is to change yourself and you'll understand what little chance you have of trying to change others.

Jacob Braude

What the mother sings to the cradle goes all the way down to the coffin.

Henry Ward Beecher

To reform a man, you must begin with his grandmother.
Victor Hugo

Consider the two levers for moving men: interest and fear.

Napoleon Bonaparte

You cannot teach a man anything; you can only help him find it within himself.

Galileo Galilei

More are taken in by hope than by cunning.

Luc Vauvenargues

Never tell people how to do things. Tell them what to do, and they will surprise you with their ingenuity.

George S. Patton

Thoughts corrupt language, and language can also corrupt thought.

George Orwell

Once you believe something is true, whether or not it is, you will act as if it is.

Anonymous

I know how to listen when clever men are talking. That is the secret of what you call my influence.

Hermann Sudermann

He who influences the thoughts of his times influences the times that follow.

Elbert Hubbard

A wise man is superior to any insults which may be put upon him.

Moliere

Insults should be well-avenged or well-endured.

Spanish Proverb

An injury is much sooner forgotten than an insult.

Lord Chesterfield

If I have said something to hurt a man once, I shall not get the better of this by saying many things to please him.

Samuel Johnson

No one can be as calculatedly rude as the British, which amazes Americans, who do not understand studied insult and can only offer abuse as a substitute.

Paul Gallico

Insults

There are two insults which no human will en-
dure: the assertion that he hasn't a sense of
humor, and the doubly impertinent assertion
that he has never known trouble.

Sinclair Lewis

Think twice before you speak, and then you may
be able to say something more insulting than if
you spoke right out at once.

Evan Esar

The best way to procure an insult is to submit to
them.
William Hazlitt

If you can't ignore an insult, top it; if you can't
top it, laugh it off; and if you can't laugh it off,
it's probably deserved.

Russell Lynes

Always be a little kinder than necessary.

James M. Barrie

Remember, you show courtesy to others not because they are gentlemen, but because you are one.

Unknown

Kindness... loving people more than they deserve.

Joseph Joubert

Do not ask me to be kind; just ask me to act as though I were.

Jules Renard

Be kind; everyone you meet is fighting a hard battle.

John Watson

Kindness

One can always be kind to people one cares
nothing about.

Oscar Wilde

Kindness is something you can't give away since
it always comes back.

Anonymous

The greatest pleasure I know is to do a kind
deed by stealth and have it found out by
accident.

Charles Lamb

We cannot always oblige, but we can speak
obligingly.

Voltaire

Let us be kinder to one another.

Aldous Huxley's
last words

He was so kind, he would have held an umbrella over a duck in a shower of rain.

Douglas Jerrold

You can get more with a kind word and a gun than with just a kind word.

Johnny Carson

All doors open to courtesy.

Thomas Fuller

A kind heart is a fountain of gladness, making everything in its vicinity freshen into smiles.

Washington Irving

We hate the kindness which we don't understand.

Henry David Thoreau

Kindness

If you're naturally kind, you attract a lot of
people you don't like.

William Feather

In human relations kindness and lies are worth
a thousand truths.

Graham Greene

Three things in human life are important. The
first is to be kind. The second is to be kind.
And the third is to be kind.

Henry James

A kind word to one in trouble is often like a
switch in a railroad track... an inch between
wreck and smooth sailing.

Henry Ward Beecher

A lot of people think that if they are kind, somebody will take advantage of them, and sometimes they are right.

Don Herold

People are sometimes the kindest to those they want to deceive.
> Ben Hecht

Forgiveness is a way we can alter the past.

> David Bella

Good words cost no more than bad.

> Thomas Fuller

The most precious thing anyone, man or business, anybody or anything, can have is the goodwill of others.
> Anne Parish

Kindness in words creates confidence.
Kindness in thinking creates profoundness.
Kindness in giving creates love.

> Lao-Tse

Two great talkers will not travel far.

George Borrow

People will listen a great deal more patiently
while you explain your mistakes than when you
explain your successes.

Wilbur N. Nesbit

No man would listen to you if he didn't know it
was his turn next.

E. W. Howe

The opposite of talking isn't listening. The
opposite of talking is waiting.

Fran Lebowitz

There is nothing like listening to show you that
the world outside your head is different from the
one inside your head.

Thornton Wilder

Education is the ability to listen to almost anything without losing your temper or self-confidence.

> Robert Frost

If you really listen, you will hear people repeating themselves. You will hear their pleading natures or their attaching natures or their asserting natures.

> Gertrude Stein

Everything has been said before, but since nobody listens we have to keep going back and saying it all over again.

> Andre Gide

He understands badly who listens badly.

> Welsh Proverb

The quieter you become the more you can hear.

> Proverb

Listening

When you talk you only say something that you already know; when you listen you learn what someone else knows.

Anonymous

A good listener is like a catcher in baseball. He keeps tossing the ball back for you to pitch.

Franklin P. Jones

No one really listens to anyone else, and if you try it for a while you'll see why.

Mignon McLaughlin

Always listen to the opinions of others; it probably won't do you any good, but it will others.

Anonymous

Talk is cheap because the supply exceeds the demand.

Anonymous

The reason why we have two ears and only one tongue is so we may listen more and talk less.

Diogenes

It's better for things to go in one ear and out the other than to go in one ear, get all mixed up, and then slip out of the mouth.

Anonymous

One way to be popular is to listen attentively to a lot of things you already know.

Unknown

I know you believe you understand what you think I said, but I am not sure you realize that what you heard is not what I meant.

Unknown

Listening

From listening comes wisdom and from speaking repentance.

Italian Proverb

A bore is a person who talks when you wish him to listen.

Ambrose Bierce

You must know you don't know before you will listen.

Anonymous

While the right to talk may be the beginning of freedom, the necessity of listening is what makes that right important.

Walter Lippman

When all men speak, no man hears.

Proverb

No man ever listened himself out of a job.

> Calvin Coolidge

Nothing derails a train of thought more effectively than listening to a person with a one-track mind.

> Anonymous

If you can't get people to listen to you any other way, tell them it is confidential.

> Farmer's Digest

The first duty of love is to listen.

> Paul Tillich

Nothing is more common than for men to think that because they are familiar with words they understand the ideas they stand for.

> Cardinal John Newman

Listening

Give every man thy ear, but few thy voice.

William Shakespeare

An open ear is the only believable sign of an open heart.

David Augsburger

That man's silence is wonderful to listen to.

Thomas Hardy

Whatever the self describes, describes the self.

Jacob Boehme

Our dignity lies in our doubt.

Unknown

Waiting for some people to stop talking is like looking for the end of a roller towel.

Anonymous

Far too many of us listen to a new idea with our prejudices.

Anonymous

If a man could keep his trap shut, the world would beat a path to his door.

Franklin P. Adams

Nothing makes you a better listener than hearing your name mentioned.

Anonymous

Every time a man unburdens his heart to a listening stranger he reaffirms the love that unites humanity.

Germaine Greer

We frequently forgive those who bore us, but cannot forgive those whom we bore.

> La Rochefoucauld

Examine what is said, not him who speaks.

> Arabian Proverb

Listening is a very dangerous thing. If one listens, one may be convinced.

> E. M. Forster

Listen twice before you speak once.

> Proverb

You can unlock a man's whole life if you listen to what words he uses most.

> William Drummond

Necessity never made a good bargain.

Benjamin Franklin

The man who is most slow in promising is most sure to keep his word.

Jean Jacques Rousseau

Ask too much to get enough.

Spanish Proverb

Most of us know how to say nothing; few of us know when.

Anonymous

Men who differ in principles cannot help each other in their plans.

Anonymous

Negotiation

It is better to be defeated on principle than to win on lie.

Arthur Caldwell

You can't make wrong work.

Gerald Waterhouse

Negotiation in the classic diplomatic sense assumes both parties are more anxious to agree than disagree.

Dean Acheson

Hearts may agree though the heads differ.

Proverb

I cannot give you a formula for success, but I can give you the formula for failure - which is: "Try to please everybody."

Herbert Bayard Swope

The ability to see the situation as the other side sees it is one of the most important skills a negotiator can possess.

Roger Fisher

The spider and the fly can't make a bargain.

Jamaican Proverb

Give to every other human being every right that you claim for yourself.
Robert Ingersoll

Prefer a loss to a dishonest gain; the one brings pain at the moment, the other for all time.

Chilon

Any idea held by a person that was not put in by reason cannot be taken out by reason.

Kenneth D. Naden

Negotiation

When a man tells me he's going to put all his
cards on the table, I always look up his sleeve.

Lord Hore-Belisha

We can send a message around the world in 30
seconds, but it sometimes takes years to get an
idea through a quarter inch of skull.

Anonymous

Hay is more acceptable to an ass than gold.

Latin Proverb

I can forget and you can forget, but a piece of
paper never forgets.

Anonymous

A verbal contract isn't worth the paper it's
written on.

Louis B. Mayer

It is important to let people know what you stand for. It's equally important that they know what you won't stand for.

B. Bader

The earth has enough for every man's need, but not for every man's greed.

Mahatma Gandhi

Ambition is like hunger, it obeys no law but its appetite.

H. W. Shaw

Better a friendly refusal than an unwilling promise.

German Proverb

If all else fails, lower your standards.

Anonymous

Negotiation

Don't shake hands too eagerly

> Greek Proverb

We cannot negotiate with those who say, "what's mine is mine, what's yours is negotiable".

> John F. Kennedy

With someone who holds nothing but trump, it is impossible to play.
> Friedrich Hubbel

Do not expect justice where might is right.

> Phaedrus

Everybody's negotiable.

> Muhammad Ali

The fellow who agrees with everything you say is either a fool, or he is getting ready to skin you.

Frank M. Hubbard

Flattery is the infantry of negotiation.

Lord Chandos

Once the toothpaste is out of the tube, it's hard to get it back in.
H. R. Haldeman

Time is the wisest counselor.

Pericles

Negotiation lies in finding out what the other person really wants and showing him a way to get it, while you get what you want.

Herb Cohen

Her thin figure stiffened into an exclamation
point of disapproval.

> Joseph C. Lincoln

She reads my silence like a page.

> Robert Campbell

The right word may be effective, but no word
was ever as effective as a rightly timed pause.

> Mark Twain

She looked at him as if he were something she
had stepped in.
> Anonymous

May my silence become more accurate.

> Theodore Roethke

A look passed between them, like a silent exchange of two doctors who agree on a simple diagnosis without having to put it into words.

Marilyn Sharp

He glared at me like a wolf in a trap.

Robert Traver

The face is the index of the mind.

Proverb

An eye can threaten like a loaded and levelled gun, or it can insult like hissing or kicking, or, in its altered mood, by beams of kindness, it can make the heart dance with joy.

Ralph Waldo Emerson

Non-Verbal Communication

Men trust their ears less than their eyes.

Herodotus

I hate the giving of the hand unless the whole
man accompanies it.

Ralph Waldo Emerson

At fifty, everyone has the face he deserves.

George Orwell

Nature gives you your face, but you have to
provide the expression.

Unknown

He had received the news from her eyebrows.

John Galsworthy

He would not blow his nose without moralizing on conditions in the hankerchief business.

Cyril Connolly

When all agree in opinion, it's not too long before they're wrong.

Proverb

A man who is always ready to believe what is told of him will never do well.

Petronius

A belief is not merely an idea the mind possesses; it is an idea that possesses the mind.

Robert Bolton

Let us always remember that he does not really believe his own opinions who dares not give free scope to his oponent.

Wendell Phillips

The most difficult secret for a man to keep is his own opinion of himself.

> Marcel Pagnol

Nothing is more conducive to peace of mind than not having any opinion at all.

> G. C. Lichtenberg

Opinion is holding something to be provisionally true which you do not know to be false.

> Saint Bernard

Opinions have vested interests just as men have.

> Samuel Butler

Modesty in delivering our opinions leaves us the liberty of changing them without humiliation.

> Anonymous

Judge men not by their opinions, but by what their opinions have made of them.

G. C. Lichtenberg

Every opinion uttered from one's mouth is autobiographical.

Mark Ortman

There is no greater mistake than the hasty conclusion that opinions are worthless because they are bady argued.

Thomas Huxley

The foolish and the dead never change their opinions.

James Russell Lowell

People do not seem to realize that their opinions of the world are also a confession of character.

Ralph Waldo Emerson

Opinions

Opinion is something wherein I go about to give reason why all the world should think as I think.

John Selden

Opinions cannot survive if one has no chance to fight for them.

Thomas Mann

Opinion is ultimately determined by the feelings, and not by the intellect.

Herbert Spencer

Popular opinion is the greatest lie in the world.

Thomas Fuller

The average man's opinions are much less fool-ish than they would be if he thought for himself.

Bertrand Russell

A man who never alters his opinion is like standing water, and breeds reptiles of the mind.

William Blake

I must respect the opinions of others even though I disagree with them.

Herbert Henry Lehman

Every new opinion, at its starting, is precisely a minority of one.

Thomas Carlyle

Even good opinions are worth very little unless we hold them in a broad, intelligent and spacious way.

John Morley

It were not best that we should all think alike; it is difference of opinion that makes horse-races.

Mark Twain

Opinions

Everyone has the right to hold opinions without interference and to seek, receive and impart information and ideas through any media regardless of frontiers.

> Universal Declaration of
> Human Rights

Risk little on the opinion of a man who has nothing to lose.

> Anonymous

Inconsistencies of opinion, arising from changes of circumstances are often justifiable.

> Daniel Webster

He never chooses an opinion; he just wears whatever happens to be in style.

> Leo Tolstoy

We are all more or less slaves of our opinions.

> William Hazlitt

A narrow mind and a wide mouth usually go together.

Anonymous

Some people strengthen the society just by being the kind of people they are.

John W. Gardner

A man who finds no satisfaction in himself, seeks for it in vain elsewhere.

La Rochefoucauld

In great matters people show themselves as they wish to be seen; in small matters, as they are.

Gamaliel Bradford

The meeting of two personalities is like the contact of two chemical substances... if there are any reactions, both are transformed.

Carl G. Jung

Tolerance often gets the credit that belongs to indifference.

> Anonymous

Mistrust your zeal for doing good for people.

> Abbe Havelin

I'm learning about people the hard way, by being one.

> Ashleigh Brilliant

To expect common sense from people proves you're lacking it yourself.

> Eugene O'Neill

People who carved out a place in history didn't do it by chiseling.

> Anonymous

We find it hard to believe that other people's thoughts are as silly as our own, but they probably are.

James Harvey Robinson

The accent of one's birthplace lingers in the mind and in the heart as it does in one's speech.

La Rochefoucauld

Everyone is a prisoner of his own experiences. No one can eliminate prejudices, just recognize them.

Edward R. Murrow

People can put up with almost anything if they can see the reason for it.

Bruno Bettelheim

Whatever you may be sure of, be sure of this: that you are dreadfully like other people.

Amy Lowell

Our world is made up of protons, electrons, neutrons and morons.

Unknown

We do not see things as they are; we see things as we are.

The Talmud

If a man does not keep pace with his companions, perhaps it is because he hears a different drummer. Let him step to the music that he hears, however measured or far away.

Henry David Thoreau

As the sun is best seen at its rising and setting, so men's native dispositions are clearest seen when they are children and when they are dying.

Robert Boyle

Two men look through the same bars; one sees the mud, and the other the stars.

Frederick Langbridge

A human being is a creature that can't get its toes in its mouth after babyhood, but can put its foot in at anytime.

Anonymous

Silent men, like still waters, are deep and dangerous.

H. G. Bohn

Do you wish to find out a person's weak points? Note the failings he has the quickest eye for in others.

A. H. Hare

A liberal is a person whose interests aren't at stake at the moment.

Willis Player

There are three classes of people: lovers of wisdom, lovers of humor, lovers of gain.

Plato

The trouble with most people is that they think with their hopes or fears or wishes rather than with their minds.

Will Durant

A liar is a person with no partition between his imagination and his information.

Anonymous

What he lacks in intelligence, he makes up for in stupidity.

Anonymous

What matters is not the idea a person holds, but the depth at which he holds it.

Erza Pound

It is absurd to divide people into good and bad.
People are either charming or tedious.

Oscar Wilde

Everything living forms an atmosphere around
itself.

Goethe

In spite of everything I still believe that people
are really good at heart.

Anne Frank

There are no perfect human beings, and there
never will be.

Henry Miller

Everybody is all right, really.

Winnie the Pooh
(Related by A.A. Milne)

Persuasiveness

People don't ask for facts in making up their minds. They would rather have one good soul satisfying emotion than a dozen facts.

Robert Keith Leavitt

One can never understand that which he cannot see.

Anonymous

People can be induced to swallow anything, provided it is seasoned with praise.

Moliere

An idea isn't responsible for the people who believe in it.

Don Marquis

To get others to come to our way of thinking, we must go over to theirs. And it is necessary to follow in order to lead.

William Hazlitt

If you want to gather honey, don't kick over the bee hive.

Dale Carnegie

Some things have to be believed to be seen.

Anonymous

To persuade is more trouble than to dominate, and the powerful seldom take this trouble if they can avoid it.

Charles Horton Cooley

Always think in terms of what the other person wants.

James Van Fleet

If you would convince a man that he does wrong, do right. Men will believe what they see.

Henry David Thoreau

Persuasiveness

A man in the wrong may more easily be convinced than one half right.

Ralph Waldo Emerson

The object of oratory is not truth, but persuasion.

Thomas Macaulay

We do not handle people by defeat, but by persuasion.

Anonymous

If you can't convince them, confuse them.

Harry S. Truman

Crafty men deal in generalizations.

Proverb

If you persuade, speak of interest, not reason.

Benjamin Franklin

A drop of honey catches more flies than a gallon of gall.

Abraham Lincoln

The best way to convince a fool is to let him have his own way.

Josh Billings

A lot of words get spilled as the urge to be understood clashes with an aversion to being understood too well.

Anonymous

Blessed are they who have nothing to say and cannot be persuaded to say it.

Anonymous

Persuasiveness

One of the best ways to persuade others is with your ears, by listening.

Dean Rusk

You can preach a better sermon with your life than with your lips.
Oliver Goldsmith

The desire to seem clever often keeps us from being so.
La Rochefoucauld

One half of our troubles of this life can be traced to saying yes too soon or saying no too soon.

Josh Billings

Charm is a way of getting the answer "yes" without having asked any clear questions.

Albert Camus

Everything that deceives may be said to enchant.
>
> Plato

A hustler is a man who will talk you into giving him a free ride and make it seem as if he is doing you a great favor.

> Bill Veeck

If what we say to people does not tie in quickly and easily with their interest and experience, they will ignore it altogether.

> Unknown

When a person tells you, "I'll think it over and let you know"... you know.
>
> Olin Miller

Reasonable men are open to persuasion.

> Plutarch

Make it easy for people to do the things you suggest.

Anonymous

Tyrants have not yet discovered any chains that can fetter the mind.

C. C. Colton

To please people is the greatest step toward persuading them.

Lord Chesterfield

It is not what we say that counts, it is what they believe of what we say that really counts.

Anonymous

When a man is trying to sell you something, don't believe he is that polite all the time.

E. W. Howe

Most people have ears but few have good judgment; tickle those ears and you will persuade their judgment.

Anonymous

People are generally better persuaded by the reasons which they have themselves discovered than by those which come from the minds of others.

Blaise Pascal

No man should act as to make a gain off the ignorance of others.

Cicero

A silent man is not a conquered man.

Russian Proverb

There is always free cheese in a mousetrap.

Proverb

Placing Blame

When you point your finger at someone else, you have three fingers pointed at yourself.

> Lewis Mizer

A clear conscience laughs at false accusations.

> English Proverb

A man can fail many times but he isn't a failure until he begins to blame somebody else.

> Anonymous

Few blame themselves until they have exhausted all other possibilities.

> Anonymous

Don't kill the donkey unless you're ready to carry the load.

> Anonymous

We blame in others only those faults by which
we do not profit.
>Alexander Dumas

One must never excuse oneself by pointing to
the soldiers.
>Blaise Montlue

It is not whether you win or lose, but how you
place the blame.
>Anonymous

Do not blame what cannot be changed.

>Publilius Syrus

There is a luxury in self reproach. When we
blame ourselves we feel no one else has a right
to blame us.
>Oscar Wilde

Praise

Among the smaller duties of life, I hardly know
any one more important than that of praising
where praise is due.

Sydney Smith

The refusal of praise is a wish to be praised
twice.

La Rochefoucauld

Be quick to praise people. People like to praise
those who praise them.

Bernard M. Baruch

The sweetest sound of all sounds is praise.

Xenophon

He who praises another enriches himself far
more than he does the one praised. The poorest
human being has something to give that the
richest could not buy.

George Matthew Adams

Praise does wonders for our sense of hearing.

Arnold H. Glasow

A true friend is someone who says nice things behind your back.

Anonymous

Get someone to blow your own horn and the sound will carry twice as far.

Will Rogers

The meanest and most contemptible kind of praise is that which first speaks well of a man, then qualifies it with a "but".

Henry Ward Beecher

Old praise dies unless you feed it.

English Proverb

Great tranquility of heart is his who cares for
neither praise nor blame.

Thomas a' Kempis

Some natures are too good to be spoiled by
praise.

Ralph Waldo Emerson

Praise shames me, for I secretly beg for it.

Rabindranath Tagore

Modesty is the only sure bait when you angle for
praise.

Lord Chesterfield

Anything scarce is valuable; praise for example.

Anonymous

Sincere praise reassures individuals. It helps them neutralize doubts they have about themselves.

> Anonymous

Oh, how criticism undermines people's motivation, and praise promotes achievement.

> Anonymous

We should give as we would receive, cheerfully, quickly, and without hesitation; for there is no grace in a benefit that sticks to the fingers.

> Seneca

The advantage of doing one's praising to oneself is that one can lay it on so thick and exactly in the right places.

> Samuel Butler

Stand up to be seen; speak up to be heard; shut up to be appreciated.

> Unknown

Speech is power, speech is to persuade, to convert, to compel.

> Ralph Waldo Emerson

Nothing is so unbelievable that oratory cannot make it acceptable.

> Cicero

Once you get them laughing and their mouths open, you can stuff anything in.

> Francis Harvey Green

There are some people who speak well but write badly. A reason, the audience and the situation stimulate them to draw from their minds more than they could think of without such a challenge.

> Blaise Pascal

Oratory is like prostitution: you have to share a few tricks.

Vittorio Orlando

In oratory the greatest art is to hide the art.

Jonathan Swift

One of the most important ingredients in a recipe for speechmaking is plenty of shortening.

Anonymous

What oratory lacks in depth it makes up in length.

Charles L. Montesquieu

To speak logically, prudently and adequately is a talent few possess.

Michel de Montaigne

Public Speaking

Public speaking is the art of diluting a two-minute idea with a two-hour vocabulary.

Evan Esar

I have never failed to convince an audience that the best thing they could do was to go away.

Thomas Love Peacock

If you have to make an unpopular speech, give it all the sincerity you can muster; that's the only way to sweeten it.

Cardinal Jean de Retz

A speech is like a bad tooth; the longer it takes to draw out, the more it hurts.

W. E. Suter

Talking and eloquence are not the same: a fool may talk, but a wise man speaks with eloquence.

Ben Johnson

My father gave me three hints in public speaking: be sincere, be brief and be seated.

James Roosevelt

In preparing a speech, remember to make brief notes; Abraham Lincoln wrote the Gettysburg Address on the back of an envelope.

Unknown

Lecturer: One with his hand in your pocket, his tongue in your ear, and his faith in your patience.

Ambrose Bierce

Orator: A man who is willing to lay down your life for his country.

Anonymous

The man with power but no conscience, could, with an eloquent tongue, put the whole country into flames.

Woodrow Wilson

Public Speaking

I remember my lesson from the horse and buggy days. The longer the spoke the bigger the tire.

Anonymous

Speeches are like steer horns... a point here, a point there, and a lot of bull in between.

John Morley

Speakers are most vehement when their cause is weak.

Cicero

A speech is like a love affair. Any fool can start it, but to end it requires considerable skill.

Lord Mancroft

If you haven't struck oil in the first three minutes, stop boring.

George Jessel

In difficulty you understand your friends.

Chinese Proverb

A disagreement may be the shortest cut between two minds.

Kahlil Gibran

When a situation becomes hopeless, there's nothing to worry about.

Edward Abby

Instead of putting others in their place, put yourself in their place.

Anonymous

What can the enemy do when the friend is cordial?

Persian Proverb

Never cut what you can untie.

Joseph Joubert

To every action there is always opposed and equal reaction.

Isaac Newton

The removal of human friction is 90% of the problem of handling people.

Anonymous

A chip on the shoulder is about the heaviest load that anyone can carry.

Unknown

I always saw better when my eyes were closed.

Tom Waits

Don't fight a battle if you don't gain anything by winning.

> Gen. George S. Patton

Do not fight too often with your enemy, or you will teach him all your art of war.

> Napoleon Bonaparte

After a storm comes a calm.

> Proverb

Do not think of knocking out another person's brains because he differs in opinion from you. It would be as rational to knock yourself on the head because you differ from yourself ten years ago.

> Horace Mann

Humour is really laughing off a hurt.

> Bill Mauldin

Resolving Conflict

The remedy for injuries is not to remember
them.

Italian Proverb

When things go wrong, don't go with them.

Anonymous

Follow the first law of holes: if you're in one,
stop digging.

Dennis Healey

Am I not destroying my enemies when I make
friends of them?

Abraham Lincoln

Birds sing after a storm; why shouldn't we?

Rose Kennedy

When I refuse to forgive, I am burning a bridge that someday I may need to pass over.

Josh McDowell

Never "for the sake of peace and quiet" deny your convictions.

Dag Hammarskjold

To live happily with other people, ask of them only what they can give.

Tristan Bernard

Your understandings are the misunderstandings.

St. Francis of Assisi

We would often be ashamed of our finest actions if the world understood our motives.

La Rochefoucauld

The deeper the sorrow, the less tongue it has.

The Talmud

A simple rule in dealing with someone who is hard to get along with is to remember that this person is striving to assert his superiority; and you must deal with him from that point of view.

Alfred Adler

Two persons cannot long be friends if they cannot forgive each other's little failings.

Jean de La Bruyere

Peace begins where ambition ends.

Edward Young

Adversity introduces a man to himself.

Anonymous

It isn't your position that makes you happy or unhappy. It's your disposition.

Anonymous

Happiness is a conscious choice, not an automatic response.

Mildred Barthel

Grief is not in the nature of things, but an opinion.

Cicero

Even a sheet of paper has two sides.

Anonymous

Men are disturbed, not by the things that happen, but by their opinion of the things that happen.

Epictetus

Resolving Conflict

It is the way we react to circumstances that
determine our feelings.

Dale Carnegie

If you live in the river you should make friends
with the crocodiles.

Indian Proverb

No man can think clearly when his fists are
clenched.

George Jean Nathan

When you're up to your nose in it, keep your
mouth shut.

Jack Beauregard

Remember, there are small Hilter's busy around
us every day.

Anonymous

People do things for their reasons, not yours.

Unknown

A man will fight harder for his interests than his rights.

Napoleon Bonaparte

People are not against you, they are merely for themselves.

Gene Fowler

The heart has its reasons, which reason does not understand.

Blaise Pascal

All we do is done with an eye to something else.

Aristotle

Human history is the sad result of each one
looking out for himself.

Julio Cortazar

A man always has two reasons for doing
anything: a good reason and the real reason.

J. P. Morgan

Yield to a man's taste and he will yield to your
interests.
Lord Lytton

It is not true that every man has his price. But
for every man there exists a bait which he cannot resist swallowing.

Friedrich Nietzsche

The difficulty is to know conscience from self
interests.
W.D. Howells

Conscience whispers, but interest speaks aloud.

J. Petit-Senn

Talk to a man about himself and he will listen for hours.

Benjamin Disraeli

Talk in terms of the other person's interest.

Dale Carnegie

We would frequently be ashamed of our good deeds if people saw all of the motives that produced them.

La Rochefoucauld

We go on fancying that every man is thinking of us, but he is not; he is like us; he is thinking of himself.

Charles Reade

He that has satisfied his own thirst turns his
back on the well.

La Rochefoucauld

Self-preservation is nature's first law.

Thomas Fuller

Everyone thinks chiefly of his own, hardly ever
of public interest.

Aristotle

Every human being is treacherous to every other
human being because he has to be true to his
own soul.

D. H. Lawrence

Everybody acts not only under external compulsion but also in accordance with inner necessity.

Albert Einstein

If we do not take care of ourselves first, we become useless in helping others.

Anonymous

He who lives only to benefit himself confers on the world a benefit when he dies.

Tertullian

Self interest is a vice which no one will forgive in others, but which everyone forgives in himself.

Unknown

Selfishness is when someone places his own comfort before your convenience.

Joan Tepperman

Everyone has his reasons.

Jean Renoir

Silence

I have often regretted my speech, never my silence.

> Publilius Syrus

What you don't see with your eyes, don't witness with your mouth.

> Jewish Proverb

Silence is sometimes the answer.

> Estonian Proverb

If you don't say anything, you won't be called to repeat it.

> Calvin Coolidge

The reason some people suffer in silence is because sharing it would take all the pleasure out of it.

> Anonymous

In human intercourse the tragedy begins, not when there is misunderstanding about words, but when silence is not understood.

Henry David Thoreau

Silence is the only thing that cannot be mis-quoted.

Evan Esar

Silence is the fence around wisdom.

Hebrew Proverb

Silence is wisdom's best reply.

Euripides

Silence is a friend who never betrays.

Confucius

I have never been hurt by anything I didn't say.

Calvin Coolidge

The silent will be no witness against themselves.

Alfred De Vigny

Her silence bore down on him like a tombstone.

Heinrich Boll

The silence of pure innocence often persuades
when speaking fails.
William Shakespeare

Sooner or later, some of us will have to buy an
instrument that can switch on silence instead of
sound.
J. B. Priestley

Who then tells a finer tale than any of us...
silence does.

                          Isak Dinesen

There is no reply so sharp as silent contempt.

                          Michel de Montaigne

Silence is one great art of conversation.

                          William Hazlitt

Silence is the ultimate weapon of power.

                          Charles De Gaulle

Silence is one of the hardest arguments to
refute.

                          Josh Billings

The world would be happier if men had the same capacity to be silent that they have to speak.

Baruch Spinoza

He had occasional flashes of silence that made his conversation perfectly delightful.

Sydney Smith

May my silence be more accurate.

Theodore Roethke

Silence is foolish if we are wise, but wise if we are foolish.

C. C. Colton

Sometimes silence is not golden, just yellow.

Anonymous

Wrinkles should merely indicate where smiles have been.
>   Mark Twain

A smile is a light on your face to let others know you are home.

>   Anonymous

It takes 72 muscles to frown, but only 16 to smile; so if you are tired, smile.

>   Unknown

The man who smiles when things go wrong has thoughts of someone he can blame it on.

>   Anonymous

He smiled like a wolf at the thought of the next meal.
>   Mike Fredman

Smiling

The teeth are smiling, but is the heart?

                Congolese Proverb

The way you smile, with your whole face, with your eyes; it's like a certificate of trust.

                T. Coraghessan Boyle

Smiles form the channel of a future tear.

                Lord Byron

A smile is such a powerful weapon that you can even break ice with it.

                Anonymous

All people still smile in the same language.

                Proverb

Tact is the knack of making a point without making an enemy.

Howard W. Newton

Some people have tact, others tell the truth.

Virginia Pilot

Tact is the ability to make your guests feel at home where you wish they were.

Anonymous

If you wouldn't write it and sign it, don't say it.

Earl Wilson

I do not object to people looking at their watches when I am speaking, but I do strongly object when they start shaking them to make certain they are still going.

Lord Birkett

Tact

Tact is the art of building a fire under people without making their blood boil.

> Anonymous

Tact is the art of convincing people that they know more than you know.

> Raymond Mortimer

Be honest with yourself, but tactful with others.

> Henry Rabin

A slip of the foot you may soon recover, but a slip of the tongue you may never get over.

> Unknown

Better slip with the foot than with the tongue.

> Proverb

It is bad manners to begin courting a widow
before she gets home from the funeral.

Seumas MacManus

Tact is the fine art of not saying what you think.

Franklin P. Jones

Tact is changing the subject without changing
your mind.

Anonymous

Good breeding consists in concealing how much
we think of ourselves and how little we think of
the other person.

Mark Twain

Tact is the ability to close your mouth before
someone else wants to.

Anonymous

Tact

Tact in audacity is knowing how far you can go without going too far.

Jean Cocteau

Silence is not always tact and it is tact that is golden, not silence.

Samuel Butler

Tact is the art of making a point without making an enemy.

Anonymous

It is bad judgment to speak of halters in the house of a man who has been hanged.

Miguel De Cervantes

When you go to a donkey's house, don't talk about ears.

Jamaican Proverb

I've found that people who talk a lot are doing what they do best.

Anonymous

Talking without thinking is like shooting without aiming.

Anonymous

Be sure the brain is in gear before putting your mouth in motion.

Unknown

Oh Lord, please fill my mouth with worthwhile stuff, and nudge me when I've said enough.

Anonymous

Remember, a closed mouth gathers no feet.

Steve Post

Talking

Another thing a man can do that the lower
animals can't is stand upright in front of
a crowd and put both feet in his mouth.

Anonymous

It is so simple to be wise. Just think of something stupid, then say the opposite.

Sam Levenson

Keep the golden mean between saying too much
and too little.

Publilius Syrus

I really didn't say everything I said.

Yogi Berra

Wise men talk because they have something
to say; fools talk because they want to say
something.

Plato

Never fail to know that if you are doing all the talking, you are boring somebody.

Helen Gurley Brown

Talk from personal experience; then you will be authentic.

Ben Weininger

If you can talk brilliantly about a problem, you can create the consoling illusion that it has been mastered.

Stanley Kubrick

I am a master of everything I can explain.

Theodore Haecker

The luckiest insolvent in the world is the man whose expenditure of speech is too great for his income of ideas.

Christopher Morley

193

Talking

Before you speak, you are a master of what you say; afterwards a slave.

Anonymous

An afterthought is a tardy sense of prudence that prompts one to try to shut his mouth about the time he has put his foot into it.

Gideon Wurdz

Watch your own speech, and notice how it is guided by less conscious purposes.

George Eliot

It is a luxury to be understood.

Ralph Waldo Emerson

Never speak more clearly than you think.

Jeremy Bernstein

Confessions may be good for the soul, but they are bad for the reputation.

Thomas Dewar

Before a man speaks it is always safe to assume that he is a fool. After he speaks, it is seldom necessary to assume.

H. L. Mencken

Speech was given to man to disguise his thoughts.

C. M. De Talleyrand

It is wiser to choose what to say than to say what you choose.

Anonymous

When I think over what I said, I envy dumb people.

Seneca

Talking

Talk is cheap, until you hire a lawyer.

> Anonymous

Talking to some people is like opening a new
bottle of ketchup; you gotta wait a while before
anything comes out.
> Jonathan Valin

He chattered like one to whom talking was a new
accomplishment.
> Calder Willingham

You don't have to blow out the other fellow's
light to let your own shine.

> Bernard Baruch

He had a tongue that flapped like a banner in
the wind.
> George Garrett

Few explanations ever explained the necessity of making one.

Elbert Hubbard

A dog is not considered good because of his ability to bark and a man is not considered clever because of his ability to talk.

Chuang Tzu

A great talker; he has the knack of telling you nothing in a big way.

Moliere

He who talks much cannot talk well.

Carlo Goldoni

How can I tell what I think till I see what I say?

E. M. Forster

Talking

They always talk who never think, and who have the least to say.
>   Matthew Prior

Every sentence I utter must be understood not as an affirmation, but as a question.

>   Niels Bohr

Talking is much like playing the harp; there is as much in laying the hand on the strings to stop their vibrations as in twanging them to bring out the music.
>   Oliver Wendell Holmes

One never repents of having spoken too little but often of having spoken too much.

>   Philippe de Commynes

Talk doesn't cook rice.

>   Chinese Proverb

Man is least himself when he talks in his own person. Give him a mask and he will tell the truth.

Oscar Wilde

Truth uttered before its time is often dangerous.

Anonymous

Of course the truth hurts. You would too if you were stretched so much.

Anonymous

Better a lie that heals than a truth that wounds.

Czech Proverb

The only way to speak the truth is to speak lovingly.

Henry David Thoreau

The truth doesn't hurt unless it ought to.

B.C. Forbes

There are some people so addicted to exaggeration that they can't tell the truth without lying.

Josh Billings

He that speaks truth must first have one foot in the stirrup.
Turkish Proverb

When you shoot an arrow of truth, dip the point in honey.
Arab Proverb

It is always the best policy to tell the truth, unless of course you are an exceptionally good liar.
Jerome K. Jerome

When you tell the truth you do not have to remember what you said.

Anonymous

It is possible for one to tell you all the facts and still not all the truth.

Anonymous

It is twice as hard to crush a half-truth as a whole lie.

Wesley News

All truths are half-truths.

Alfred North Whitehead

Truth is what is left over after the prejudice, stupidity, vested interest and ulterior motives of the participant and observer have been eliminated.

Unknown

Truthfulness

Half the truth is often a great lie.

Benjamin Franklin

Convictions are more dangerous enemies of
truth than lies.
Friedrich Nietszche

I never know how much of what I say is true.

Bette Midler

Pushing any truth out very far, you are met by a
counter truth.
Henry Ward Beecher

Truth exists; only lies have to be invented.

Georges Braque

Any fool can tell the truth, but it requires a man of some sense to know how and when to lie.

Samuel Butler

It is hard to believe that a man is telling the truth when you know that you would lie if you were in his place.

H. L. Mencken

I like truth; I think mankind needs it. But without lies, humanity would die of boredom and futility.

Anatole France

I speak the truth, not quite my fill of it, but as much as I dare, and I dare a little more as I grow older.

Michel de Montaigne

The truth is the safest lie.

Anonymous

There is no such thing as absolute truth. People are less deceived by failing to see the truth than by failing to see its limits.

Senec de Meilhan

The great enemy of the truth is very often not the lie, but the myth: persistent, persuasive and unrealistic.

John F. Kennedy

The truth isn't what we say; its how we feel when we say it.

Merrit Malloy

When war is declared, truth is the first casualty.

Hiram Johnson

When in doubt, tell the truth.

Mark Twain

It is an equal failing to trust everybody as it is to trust nobody.

> English Proverb

You may be deceived if you trust too much, but you will live in torment unless you trust enough.

> Frank Crane

He who does not trust enough will not be trusted.

> Lao-Tzu

He who trusts men will make fewer mistakes than he who distrusts them.

> Camillo Covour

Distrust is the mother of safety, but must be kept out of sight.

> Thomas Fuller

The lion and the calf can lie down together but the calf won't get much sleep.

Woody Allen

Trust men and they will be true to you; treat them greatly and they will show themselves great.

Ralph Waldo Emerson

To be trusted is a greater compliment than to be loved.

George MacDonald

When a man has no reason to trust himself, he trusts in luck.

E. W. Howe

Trust everybody, but cut the cards.

Finley Peter Dunne

Wit is what we would have said had we thought of it.

> Anonymous

All wit rests on a cheerful awareness of life's incongruities.

> George Will

Wit is the salt of conversation, not the food.

> William Hazlitt

Wit consists of knowing the resemblance of things which differ and the difference of things which are alike.

> Madame de Stael

Use your wit as a shield, not a dagger.

> American Porverb

Many live by their wits, but few by their wit.

Laurence J. Peter

Wit has truth in it. Wisecracking is simply calisthenics with words.

Dorothy Parker

Wit, by itself, is of little account. It becomes of moment only when grounded on wisdom.

Mark Twain

You can pretend to be serious; you can't pretend to be witty.

Sacha Guidry

Instead of working for the survival of the fittest, we should be working for the survival of the wittiest; then we can all die laughing.

Lily Tomlin

He who laughs last... thinks slowest.

Bob Lockhart

Wit is so shining a quality that everybody admires it; most aim at it, all people fear it, and few love it unless in themselves.

Lord Chesterfield

Wit is a sword; it is meant to make people feel the point as well as see it.

G. K. Chesterton

Brevity is the soul of wit.

William Shakespere

Wit is a dangerous weapon, even to the possessor, if he knows not how to use it discreetly.

Michel de Montaigne

What's in a word? Consider the difference
between a wise guy and a wise man.

Unknown

If it takes a lot of words to say what you have in
mind, give it more thought.

Dennis Roth

Men of few words are best.

William Shakespeare

Better break your word than do worse by
keeping it.

Thomas Fuller

Great men, like nature, use simple language.

Luc de Clapiers

If you have to eat crow, eat it while it's hot.

Alben Barkley

Eating words has never given me indigestion.

Winston Churchill

Words have no wings but they can fly a thousand miles.

Korean Proverb

Words are really a mask. They rarely express the true meaning; in fact, they tend to hide it.

Hermann Hesse

Words, like nature, half reveal and half conceal the soul within.

Alfred Tennyson

Words

When you wish to instruct, be brief. Every word that is unnecessary only pours over the side of a brimming mind.

Cicero

Never say never and always avoid always.

John Hazlitt

Words divide us; actions unite us.

Unknown

When ideas fail, words come in handy.

Goethe

We would have a great many fewer disputes in the world if words were taken for what they are; as signs of our ideas only, and not for things themselves.

John Locke

The word communication comes from the Latin word "communico", meaning share.

Anonymous

Without knowing the force of words, it is impossible to know men.
Confucius

Words are, of course, the most powerful drug used by mankind.
Rudyard Kipling

Words differently arranged have different meanings and meanings differently arranged have different effects.
Blaise Pascal

Words have this immense privilege: you can take them with you.
Simone de Beauvior

Words

Man does not live by words alone despite the fact that sometimes he has to eat them.

Adlai Stevenson

Blessed is the man who having nothing to say, abstains from giving wordy evidence of the fact.

George Eliot

One word is worth a thousand pictures, if it's the right word.
Edward Abby

Words fashioned with somewhat over-precise diction are like shapes turned out by a cookie cutter.
Peter De Vries

Words are treated so often as trifles when in reality they can be more devastating than rifles.

Anonymous

Words like eyeglasses, blur everything they don't make clear.

> Joseph Joubert

He can compress the most words into the smallest idea of any man I ever met.

> Abraham Lincoln

Feelings; the hardest thing in the world to put into words.

> Jack London

Words are the things to kill time until emotions make us inarticulate.

> Arthur S. Roche

Our words misunderstand us.

> Adrienne Rich

Words

A word from the heart goes straight to the heart.

Abbe Huvelin

Better one word before than two after.

Welsh Proverb

He who does not understand your silence will probably not understand your words.

Elbert Hubbard

Not a sentence or word is independent of the circumstances under which it was uttered.

Alfred North Whitehead

The true meaning of a word is to be found by observing what a person does with it, not by what he says about it.

Anonymous

The Power of Words

A careless word may kindle strife,

A cruel word may wreck a life;

A bitter word may hate instill,

A brutal word may smite and kill.

A gracious word may smooth the way,

A joyous word may light the day;

A timely word may lessen stress,

A loving word may heal and bless.

Author Unknown

Author's Index

Abby, Edward 18, 167, 214
Aberland, Peter 34
Acheson, Dean 126
Adams, Franklin P. 123
Adams, George Matthew 158
Ade, George
Adler, Alfred 172
Aesop 14, 16
Ali, Muhammad 130
Allen, Woody 206
Amiel, Henry F. 97
Analects 91
Anderson, Sherwood 103
Ardrey, Robert 99
Arendt, C. E. 36
Aristotle 27, 89, 101, 175, 178
Assisi, St. Francis 171
Augsburger, David 122
Ayres, C. E. 36

Bacon, Francis 34
Bader, B. 129
Baker, Russell 60
Barkley, Alben 211
Barrie, James 111
Barthel, Mildred 173
Barton, Bruce 72
Baruch, Bernard M. 158, 196
Beauregard, Jack 174
Beecher, Henry Ward 107, 114, 159, 202
Bella, David 115
Bennet, W. C. 20
Benson, A. C. 19

Bernard, St. 136
Bernard, Tristen 37, 171
Bernstein, Jeremy 194
Berra, Yogi 192
Bettelheim, Bruno 143
Bhagvad Gita 99
Bible 90
Bierce, Ambrose 70, 120, 165
Billings, Josh 15, 23, 37, 42, 58, 151, 152, 183, 200
Birkett, Lord 187
Blake, William 139
Boehme, Jacob 122
Bohn, H. G. 145
Bohr, Niels 198
Boll, Heinrich 182
Bolton, Robert 135
Bonaparte, Napoleon 107, 169, 175
Borrow, George 116
Bourne, Randolph 73
Boyle, Robert 144
Boyle, T. Coraghessan 186
Bradford, Gamaliel 141
Brandeis, Louis D. 26, 27
Braude, Jacob 106
Braque, Georges 202
Brilliant, Ashleigh 142
Brown, Helen Gurley 193
Bruyere, Jean de, La 172
Buckley, Christopher 33
Burke, Edmund 42
Butler, Samuel 67, 136, 161, 190, 203
Byron, Lord (George Gordon) 18, 186

Caldwell, Arthur 126
Campbell, Robert 132
Camus, Albert 98, 152
Camus, Jean Pierre 101

Calisher, Hortense 133
Carlyle, Thomas 75, 80, 139
Carnegie, Dale 21, 24, 149, 174
Carroll, Lewis 21
Carson, Johnny 113
Cavett, Dick 60
Chandos, Lord 131
Chesterfield, Lord 109, 154, 160, 209
Chesterton, G. K. 104, 209
Chilon 127
Churchill, Winston 211
Cicero 155, 162, 166, 173, 212
Cocteau, Jean 190
Cohen, Herb 131
Coleridge, Samuel Taylor 15, 97
Collins, John Churton 64
Colton, Charles Caleb 94, 100, 154, 184
Confucius 78, 102, 104, 181, 213
Connolly, Cyril 84, 102, 135
Cooley, Charles Horton 149
Coolidge, Calvin 19, 121, 181, 182,
Cortazar, Julio 176
Covour, Camillo 205
Crane, Frank 205
Cummins, Anna 20

Dahl, Ronald 33
Danto, Arthur 15
De Beauvior, Simone 213
De Cervantes, Miguel 190
De Clapiers, Luc 210
De Commynes, Philippe 198
De Gaulle, Charles 183
De Goncourt, Jules 53
De Retz, Cardinal Jean 164
De Talleyrand, C. M. 195
De Vingny, Alfred 182

De Vries, Peter 214
Dewar, Thomas 195
Dickson, Paul 56
Dimnet, Ernest 95
Dinesen, Isak 183
Dinik, Dadistan I. 91
Diogenes 119
Disraeli, Benjamin 22, 24, 39, 51, 54, 177
Drummond, William 124
Dumas, Alexander 157
Duncan, Isadora 132
Dunne, Peter Finley 206
Durant, Will 69, 146

Edwards, Tyrone 48
Einstein, Albert 178
Eliot, George 79, 194, 214
Eliot, T. S. 63
Emerson, Ralph Waldo 40, 43, 87, 106, 133, 134, 137,
        150, 160, 162, 194, 206
Emmons, Nathanial 26
Epictetus 77, 173
Erasmus, Desiderius 36
Erhard, Ludwig 47
Esar, Evan 40, 51, 72, 82, 88, 93, 110, 164
Eschenbach, Marie von 24, 77
Euripides 181

Farmers Digest 121
Farrell, Joseph 39
Feather, William 114
Fisher, Roger 127
Fontaine, Jean D. La 81
Forbes, B.C. 200
Forbes, Malcolm 65
Forster, E. M. 124, 197
Fowler, Gene 175

France, Anatole 77, 203
Frank, Anne 147
Franklin, Benjamin 22, 64, 70, 79, 80, 88, 125, 151, 202
Fredman, Mike 185
Friedman, Sonya 16
Frost, Robert 117
Fuller, Thomas 28, 83, 86, 113, 115, 138, 178, 205, 210

Galico, Paul 109
Galileo of Galilei 107
Galloway, Dale 87
Galsworthy, John 134
Gandi, Mahatma 88, 129
Gardner, Herb 105
Gardner, John W. 141
Garrett, George 196
Giang, Vo Dong 56
Gibran, Kahlil 58, 167
Gide, Andre 101, 117
Glascow, Arnold H. 159
Glasgow, Ellen 95
Goethe, Johann Wolfgang 40, 71, 73, 74, 212
Goldberg, Isaac 69
Goldoni, Carlo 197
Goldsmith, Oliver 28, 37, 152
Goldwyn, Samuel 74
Gomez, Lefty 66
Gracian, Baltasar 30, 36
Green, Francis Harvey 162
Greene, Graham 114
Greenleaf, Stephen 134
Greer, Germaine 123
Grit 85
Guitry, Sacha 208

Haecker, Theodor 193
Hailsham, Lord 27

Haldeman, H. R. 131
Haliburton, Thomas 89
Halifax, Lord 88
Hammarskjold, Dag 171
Hardy, Thomas 122
Hare, A. H. 145
Harpe, Jean de la 61
Harper, Lucille S. 71
Harrison, Barbara G. 97
Haskins, Henry S. 14, 83
Havelin, Abe 142
Hazlitt, John 212
Hazlitt, William 52, 110, 140, 148, 183, 207
Healey, Dennis 170
Hecht, Ben 115
Heinlein, Robert 62
Herodotus 134
Herold, Don 114
Hesse, Hermann 211
Hevelin, Abbe 216
Holmes, Oliver Wendell 40, 71, 86, 100, 198
Hore-Belisha, Lord 128
Horace 89
Howard, Vernon 97
Howe, Edgar Watson 17, 20, 27, 50, 58, 116, 154, 206
Howells, W. H. 176
Hubbard, Elbert 108, 197, 216
Hubbard, Frank 131
Hubbard, Kin 36, 44, 45, 55,
Hubbel, Friedrich 130
Hugo, Victor 21, 103, 107
Huxley, Aldous 22, 112
Huxley, Thomas 137

Ingersoll, Robert 85, 127
Irving, Washington 113

Jackson, Jesse 57
James, Henry 114
James, William 21
Jarrell, Randall 58
Jefferson, Thomas 24
Jerome, Jermome K. 200
Jerome, St. 96
Jerrold, Douglas, 113
Jessell, George 166
Johnson, Ben 164
Johnson, Hiram 204
Johnson, Samuel 24, 26, 28, 48, 52, 59, 70, 101, 109
Jones, Franklin P. 59, 62, 118, 189
Joubert, Joseph 28, 111, 168, 215
Jowett, Benjamin 73
Jung, Carl G. 103, 141

Karr, Alphonse 38
Kempis, Thomas a' 78, 160
Kennedy, John F. 130, 204
Kennedy, Rose 170
Kennevan, Walter J. 33
Kipling, Rudyard 32, 213
Kirk, Lisa 52
Knox, Ronald 47
Koch, C. J. 135
Kubler-Ross, Elizabeth 39
Kubrick, Stanley 193

La Rochefoucauld, Francois 17, 43, 53, 78, 82, 124, 141,
        143, 152, 158, 171, 177, 178
Labiche, Eugene Marian 37
Lamb, Charles 112
Landers, Ann 38, 62
Langbridge, Fredrick 145
Lao-Tse 115, 205
Larson, Doug 63

Lavater, Johann Kasper 79
Lawrence, D. H. 178
Le Duc de Levis 34
Leavitt, Robert Keith 148
Lebowitz, Fran 116
Lehman, Herbert Henry 139
Lehrer, Tom 67
Leopardi, Giacomo 67
Levenson, Sam 192
Lewis, Sinclair 42, 110
Lichtenberg, G.C. 136, 137
Lincoln, Abraham 54, 151, 170, 215
Lincoln, Joseph C. 132
Lippmann, Walter 120
Lloyd, Donald 49
Locke, John 212
Lockhart, Bob 209
London, Jack 215
Longfellow, Henry Wadsworth 57
Lowell, Amy 143
Lowell, James Russell 137
Ludwig, Emil 53
Lynes, Russell 110
Lytton, Lord 176

Mac Manus, Seumas 189
Macaulay, Thomas B. 38, 150
MacDonald, George 206
Mahabbarata 90
Malloy, Merrit 204
Mancroft, Lord 166
Mann, Horace 169
Mann, Thomas 138
Marquis, Don 15, 148
Maslow, Abraham H. 106
Masson, Thomas 16, 97
Mauldin, Bill 169

Maurdis, Andre 57
Mayer, Louis B. 128
McDowell, Josh 171
McKinnon, Dan 64
McLaughlin, Mignon 118
Meilhan, Senec de 204
Mencken, H. L. 195, 203
Meredith, George 92
Metcalf, C. W. 72
Midler, Bette 202
Miller, Henry 147
Miller, Olin 153
Mizer, Lewis 156
Moliere 109, 148, 197
Montaigne, Michel de 23, 163, 183, 203, 209
Montesquieu, Charles Louis 163
Montlue, Blaise 157
Moody, D. L. 67
Morgan, J. P. 176
Morley, Christopher 193
Morley, John 105, 139, 166
Mortimer, Raymond 188
Murrow, Edward R. 143

Naden, Kenneth D. 127
Nash, Ogden 93
Needham, Richard J. 35
Nesbit, Wilbur N. 116
Nevill, Dorthy 49
Newman, Cardinal John 121
Newton, Howard W. 187
Newton, Isaac 168
Nietzsche, Friedrich Wilhelm 45, 70, 176, 202
Nixon, Richard 62

O'Casey, Sean 83
O'Neill, Eugene 142

Orben, Robert 41, 74
Orlando, Vittoria 163
Ortman, Mark 18, 24, 137
Orwell, George 108, 134
Osler, Sir William 100

P'ien, T'ai Shang Ying 91
Pagnol, Marcel 136
Palmer, Gretta 19
Parish, Anne 115
Parker, Dorothy 208
Pascal, Blaise 68, 94, 100, 155, 162, 175, 213
Patton, George S. 108, 169
Peacock, Thomas Love 164
Pearson, Hesketh 103
Pericles 131
Peter, Laurence J. 208
Petit-Senn, J. 177
Petronius 135
Phaedrus 130
Phelps, William Lyon 38
Phillips, Wendell 135
Pilot, Virginia 187
Plutarch 153
Plato 75, 146, 153, 192
Player, Willis 145
Pollan, Stephen 84
Pope, Alexander 93
Post, Dan 71
Post, Steve 191
Pound, Erza 146
Powell, John 35
Priestley, J. B. 182
Prior, Matthew 178
Prochow, Herbert 26, 29

Rabin, Henry 47, 188

Reade, Charles 177
Reerdy, Pierre 99
Renard, Jules 111
Renoir, Jean 179
Rich, Adrienne 215
Robinson, James Harvey 143
Roche, Arthur S. 215
Roethke, Theodore 132, 184
Rogers, Will 101, 159
Roosevelt, James 165
Roth, Dennis 210
Rousseau, Jean Jacques 125
Roux, Joseph 59
Rowan, Carl 31
Rusk, Dean 152
Ruskin, John 29, 70
Russell, Bertrand 63, 138

Safian, L. A. 71
Salak, J. C. 62
Santayana, George 102
Satir, Virginia 56
Schiller, Fredrich von 18
Scott, Sir Walter 39
Selden, John 138
Seneca 74, 85, 161, 195
Sertillanges, A. J. 48
Shakespeare, William 98, 122, 182, 209, 210
Sharp, Marilyn 133
Shaw, George Bernard 34, 35, 61, 81
Shaw, Herbert W. 96, 129
Sibelius, Jean 54
Sister Kenny's Mother 84
Smith, Logan Pearsell 94
Smith, Sydney 23, 184
Spencer, Herbert 139
Socrates 16

Spinoza, Baruch 184
Stael, Madame de 207
Stein, Gertrude 117
Steinbeck, John 17
Stevenson, Adlai 214
Stinnett, Caskie 68
Sudermann, Hermann 108
Sunnah 91
Suter, W.E. 164
Swift, Jonathan 50, 163
Swope, Herbert Bayard 126
Syrus, Publilius 33, 46, 86, 88, 157, 180, 192

Tagore, Rabindranath 160
The Talmud 90, 144, 172
Tarquet, Emile 44
Tennyson, Alfred 211
Tepperman, Joan 179
Tertullian 179
Thatcher, Margaret 37
Thoreau, Henry David 65, 113, 144, 149, 181, 199
Tillich, Paul 121
Tolstoy, Leo 140
Tomlin, Lily 208
Traver, Robert 133
Truman, Harry 17, 89, 104, 150
Twain, Mark 45, 46, 74, 87, 96, 132, 139, 185, 189, 204, 208
Tynan, Kenneth 54
Tzu, Chuang 197

Udanda-Varga 90

Valin, Jonathan 133, 196
Van Buran, Abigail 25
Van Der Post, Laurens 95
Van Fleet, James 149

Vauvenargues, Luc 107
Veeck, Bill 153
Voltaire 26, 32, 34, 100, 105, 112

Waits, Tom 168
Walters, Barbara 94
Walworth, Dorothy 50
Waterhouse, Gerald 126
Watson, John 111
Webster, Daniel 140
Weininger, Ben 193
Wells, Corrine V. 44
Wells, H. G. 35
Werk, Chuck 43
Wesley News 201
Whichcote, Benjamin 61
White, Betty 59
Whitehead, Alfred North 210, 216
Wilde, Oscar 18, 93, 112, 147, 157, 199
Wilder, Thorton 116
Will, George 207
Willingham, Calder 196
Wilson, Earl 35, 92, 187
Wilson, Woodrow 29, 165
Winchell, Walter 57, 93
Winnie the Pooh 147
Woolman, John 106
Wurdz, Gideon 194

Xenophon 158

ORDER FORM

To order additional copies of *Now That Makes Sense!*
send check or money order for **$11.95 U.S.** per copy with
your name address and telephone number to:

WISE OWL BOOKS
P.O. Box 621
Kirkland, WA 98083
(206) 822-9699

(Washington State residents add 8.2% sales tax)

Call if interested in distributing or quantity discounts.

- -

(Please Print)

Name: _____

Address: _____

City: _____ State: _____ Zip: _____

Phone: (_____)_____

Please send me _____ copies of *Now That Makes Sense!*

Total Amount Enclosed $ _____

Thank You!

ORDER FORM

To order additional copies of *Now That Makes Sense!*
send check or money order for **$11.95 U.S.** per copy with
your name address and telephone number to:

WISE OWL BOOKS
P.O. Box 621
Kirkland, WA 98083
(206) 822-9699

(Washington State residents add 8.2% sales tax)

Call if interested in distributing or quantity discounts.

- -
(Please Print)

Name: _____

Address: _____

City: _____ State: _____ Zip: _____

Phone: (_____)_____

Please send me _____ copies of *Now That Makes Sense!*

Total Amount Enclosed $ _____

Thank You!